West Bend
Art Museum
Collection

A Gallery
of
Great Paintings

Edited by Aimée Crane

Foreword by
PEYTON BOSWELL, JR.

CROWN PUBLISHERS
NEW YORK

CONTENTS

FOREWORD

MILLIONS upon millions of words have been written about art, due undoubtedly to the fact that, along with religion, politics and sex, art is one of the most controversial subjects relating to man's efforts to live with man. Those words have helped to spread appreciation and understanding of art; they have explained, described and dramatized artists since the first cave scratchings. And yet, through the centuries, they have never caused a bad painting to live, nor a good one to die. Today, as yesterday, the work of art itself remains the constant. If you would know art, you must look at it. There is nothing that can take the place of experiencing art at first hand — unless it is a picture book such as *A Gallery of Great Paintings*. Here, from Titian to Tchelitchew, from Bellini to Bellows, you may study at your leisure some of the world's finest paintings in their original colors.

A book like this should be taken home as one's own private gallery of paintings. While a visit to a public museum is something of a transient pleasure, a well-planned volume of color reproductions may be enjoyed at will, without the trouble of a trip beyond the library walls. It is an accessory before and after the act. Through such a medium you share with the museums and collectors the companionship of the masters, and in some minor degree feel the pride of ownership. Regarded from this angle, *A Gallery of Great Paintings* incorporates most of the factors of an important art exhibition.

Some will question the inclusion or exclusion of certain artists in this gallery-in-book-form, which is a natural attitude toward any exhibition, art being so personal in its reaction upon the individual mind and heart. However, it should be borne in mind that the editor, Aimée Crane, does not dogmatically claim to have found the 100 "best" paintings in the world. Rather, she labored to present in convenient and beautiful form typical and important examples from all schools — Italian, Dutch, Flemish, Spanish, French, German, British, American Masters, School of Paris, Abstractionists, Surrealists, and Contemporary Americans. This function she has achieved. The resulting "exhibition," borrowed from American collections with but two exceptions, has as twin keynotes variety and quality.

The Old Master section follows standard, accepted lines, containing some of the best-loved paintings in America. The Italians rank high in popular appeal, with Fra Angelico, Bellini, Botticelli, Michelangelo, Raphael, Leonardo, Perugino, Titian and Canaletto in the front ranks. There is a rare Vermeer, and an attractive pair by Rubens (the latter's "Venus and Adonis" showing to advantage the famous Fleming's full-bodied sensuality). Rembrandt, giant of them all, is seen in one of his best introspective self-portraits. The Golden Age of British paintings is represented by Gainsborough (the "Blue Boy"), Reynolds, Hoppner, Constable and Turner (with the magnificent "Fighting Temeraire"). Holbein and Van Dyck, imported by English kings, are effectively characterized, the first by strength, the other by grace. Of the immortal Spanish triumvirate, all three — El Greco, Goya and Velasquez are present.

Renoir, most painterly of the Frenchmen, has the most entries, three — all important canvasses. This section — 19th century France — is the strongest in the book, including, to mention only a few, David, Ingres, Manet, Monet, Degas, Corot, Van Gogh, Gauguin and Cézanne. Bringing the French, or Internationalist School down to our times are Matisse, Picasso, Braque (best of the Abstractionists), Rouault, Léger and Chagall (lightweight, but diverting). The sharp-focus school of pictorial expression, now gaining wide popularity following the weak contours and bleached pigment of the last decade, is epitomized by Salvador Dali (and the earlier American, William Harnett). Yves Tanguy, whom some call a Surrealist, represents the ultra-sophisticated taste of the day, aided by his opposite, the Philadelphia Negro Primitive, Horace Pippin, who has a long waiting list of theatrical celebrities anxious for his latest productions.

Approximately one-quarter of the book is devoted to American painting. Outstanding in this section is George Bellows' masterpiece, "The White Horse," indicating poignantly how severe was our loss when this great artist was so unnecessarily cut off in his prime. Other Americans to whom time has accorded the mantle of permanence are Copley, Whistler (the charming "White Girl"), Eakins, Homer, Cassatt and Sargent, whose portrait of Chase proves his power when he divorced his brush from fashion.

The contemporary Americans provide the controversial flavor. Within these pages the famous Midwest trinity of American Scene rebels — Thomas Benton, John Steuart Curry and the late Grant Wood — are once more united. These three were the partisan fighters of the late 1920's and early 1930's, whose objectives were to free native painting both from subservience to Paris and from the isolationism of the Ivory Tower. Their revolt was chiefly along the lines of subject inspiration and directness of statement. In large measure they succeeded, and the struggle which they spearheaded has now passed into American art history — just as have the chapters entitled "The Eight" and "The Armory Show." American art is more liberal today because of their efforts, and has entered its next phase, wherein the dominating accents are on paint quality, stronger design, emotional content and the other aesthetic attributes of *constructed* pictures. I have never been able to understand why the mere mention of one of the "trinity" warrants so much acrimony in certain quarters. The fact remains that no history of American art can be written without some reference to their contributions.

A reasonable prediction is that out of the Armed Forces of this war will come the artist-leaders after the Peace. And so this volume aptly casts a shadow into the future and gives space to T/Sgt. Manuel Bromberg, Cpl. Frank D. Duncan, Jr., and Ens. George F. Heuston. New, youthful vitality is bound to change the old order. Just as they will dominate the legislative halls in Washington, the returning warriors will make their impact felt on 57th Street. They are too close to the scene to paint great pictures now, but with time their thought and emotions will be clarified into a vital, authentic art.

PEYTON BOSWELL, JR.

GIOTTO, Italian 1266–1336   The Flight Into Egypt

Arena Chapel, Padua
Colorplate: Simon and Schuster   I

FRA ANGELICO, Italian 1387–1455

San Marco, Florence

The Annunciation

PERUGINO PIETRO VANNUCCI, Italian 1446–1524   Virgin in Adoration (Detail)
Pitti Palace, Florence

3

SANDRO BOTTICELLI, Italian 1447–1515
National Gallery, London

Madonna and Child

4

LEONARDO DA VINCI, Italian 1452–1519

Head of Christ

Brera Gallery, Milan

5

36

LEONARDO DA VINCI, Italian 1452–1519

Louvre, Paris

Mona Lisa

6

MICHELANGELO BUONARROTI, Italian 1475–1564　　　　Virgin and Child with St. John and Four Angels

National Gallery, London

Colorplate: Courtesy of Encyclopaedia Britannica

7

RAPHAEL, Italian 1483–1520   Madonna

Dresden Gallery, Germany
Colorplate: Courtesy of Encyclopaedia Britannica   8

TITIAN, Italian 1480–1576   Cardinal Perronot De Granvella
William Rockhill Nelson Gallery of Art, Kansas City
Colorplate: Burger-Baird Engraving Co., Kansas City   9

EL GRECO, Spanish 1541–1614   Adoration of the Shepherds   The Metropolitan Museum of Art, New York

GIOVANNI BELLINI, Italian 1428–30–1516   Portrait of a Young Man in Red
National Gallery of Art, Washington, D. C.
Colorplate: Simon and Schuster

11

TINTORETTO, Italian 1518–1594

Academy, Venice

Colorplate: Simon and Schuster

Miracle of St. Mark

PIETER BREUGHEL, Flemish 1525?–1569
The Detroit Institute of Arts
Colorplate: Simon and Schuster

The Wedding Dance

HANS HOLBEIN, German 1497–1543

Jane Seymour

Royal Museum, Vienna

FRANCISCO JOSE DE GOYA Y LUCIENTES, Spanish 1746–1828   Don Manuel Osorio De Zuñiga
Bache Collection, New York
Colorplate: Simon and Schuster

15

JOOS VAN CLEVE, Flemish 1485–1540   Madonna With the Carnation
William Rockhill Nelson Gallery of Art, Kansas City
Colorplate: Burger-Baird Engraving Co., Kansas City   16

SIR ANTHONY VAN DYCK, Flemish 1599–1641   Charles I of England

Louvre, Paris

DIEGO RODRIQUEZ DE SILVA Y VELASQUEZ, 1599–1660   Cardinal Gaspar de Boya y Velasco

The Metropolitan Museum of Art, New York

18

DIEGO RODRIQUEZ SILVA Y VELASQUEZ, Spanish 1599–1660   Infanta Maria Theresa
Museum of Fine Arts, Boston

BARTOLOME ESTEBAN MURILLO, Spanish 1618–1682   Madonna and Child
                                                                ("The Santiago Madonna")
                The Metropolitan Museum of Art, New York

20

REMBRANDT VAN RIJN, Dutch 1607–1669

National Gallery, London

Portrait of the Artist

21

Venus and Adonis

PETER PAUL RUBENS, Flemish 1577–1640
The Metropolitan Museum of Art, New York
Colorplate: Courtesy of Encyclopaedia Britannica

PETER PAUL RUBENS, Flemish 1577–1640   Wolf and Fox Hunt

The Metropolitan Museum of Art, New York

JEAN CHARDIN, French 1699–1779   The House of Cards

Louvre, Paris

24

JAN VERMEER, Dutch 1632–1675   Young Woman with a Water Jug
The Metropolitan Museum of Art, New York

LUCAS VAN LEYDEN, Dutch 1494–1533   Angel
                    Fogg Museum of Art, Harvard University
                    Grenville Lindall Winthrop Collection

Embarkation for Cythera

JEAN ANTOINE WATTEAU, French 1684–1721

Louvre, Paris

ADOLPHE WILLIAM BOUGUEREAU, French 1825–1905   Be Friends
William Rockhill Nelson Gallery of Art, Kansas City
Colorplate: Burger-Baird Engraving Co., Kansas City   28

SIR JOSHUA REYNOLDS, British 1723–1792   Viscount Althorp
Spencer Gallery, London

JEAN AUGUSTE INGRES, French 1780–1867

La Source

Louvre, Paris

FRANCOIS BOUCHER, French 1703–1770   Jupiter in the Guise of Diana and Calisto
William Rockhill Nelson Gallery of Art, Kansas City
Colorplate: Burger-Baird Engraving Co., Kansas City

THOMAS COUTURE, French 1815–1879   The Illness of Pierrot
William Rockhill Nelson Gallery of Art, Kansas City
Colorplate: Burger-Baird Engraving Co., Kansas City

THOMAS GAINSBOROUGH, British 1727–1788

Private Collection

The Blue Boy

33

JOERG BREU, German 1480–1537   Portrait of a Young Man with a Carnation
Fine Arts Gallery, San Diego   34

JOHN CONSTABLE, British 1776–1837

The Metropolitan Museum of Art, New York

Bridge on the Stour

JEAN HONORE FRAGONARD, French 1732–1806

Louvre, Paris

L'Etude

36

ANTONIO CANALETTO, Italian 1697-1768

Fogg Museum of Art, Harvard University
Grenville Lindall Winthrop Collection

Piazza San Marco

JOHN SINGER SARGENT, American 1856–1925　　　　　　　　William M. Chase
The Metropolitan Museum of Art, New York

ALEXANDER H. WYANT, American 1830–1892   Forenoon in Adirondacks

The Metropolitan Museum of Art, New York

JOHN HOPPNER, British 1758–1810   Portrait of Lady Fitzgerald
William Rockhill Nelson Gallery of Art, Kansas City
Colorplate: Burger-Baird Engraving Co., Kansas City   40

JOHN SINGLETON COPLEY, American 1737–1815   Portrait of Sir George Cooke, Bart.
William Rockhill Nelson Gallery of Art, Kansas City
Colorplate: Burger-Baird Engraving Co., Kansas City   41

GILBERT STUART, American 1755–1828   George Washington (*Carroll Portrait*)
The Metropolitan Museum of Art, New York   42

THOMAS SULLY, American 1783–1872

The Torn Hat

Museum of Fine Arts, Boston

43

WILLARD METCALF, American 1858–1925   Icebound
The Art Institute of Chicago   44

GEORGE INNESS, American 1825–1894
The Art Institute of Chicago

After a Summer Shower

GEORGE LUKS, American 1867–1933
Phillips Memorial, Washington

The Blue Devils

WINSLOW HOMER, American 1836-1910   Searchlight, Harbor Entrance, Santiago de Cuba

The Metropolitan Museum of Art, New York

JACQUES LOUIS DAVID, French 1748–1825   Mlle Charlotte Du Val D'Ognes
The Metropolitan Museum of Art, New York

48

WILLIAM M. HARNETT, American 1848–1892   For Sunday Dinner
The Downtown Gallery, New York

THOMAS EAKINS, American 1844–1916

William Rush Carving the Allegorical Figure of the Schuylkill
Brooklyn Museum, New York

JAMES WHISTLER, American 1834–1903 The White Girl National Gallery of Art, Washington, D.C.; Harris Whittemore Collection

GEORGE W. BELLOWS, American 1882–1925   The White Horse

Worcester Art Museum

JOSEPH M. W. TURNER, British 1775–1851
National Gallery, London

Fighting Temeraire

JEAN BAPTISTE COROT, French 1796–1875   The Letter
The Metropolitan Museum of Art, New York

CLAUDE MONET, French 1840–1926
The Metropolitan Museum of Art, New York

La Grenouillère

EUGENE BOUDIN, French 1824–1898   Baie de Fourmis, Beaulieu

The Metropolitan Museum of Art, New York

ODILON REDON, French 1840–1916   Vase of Flowers

William S. Paley, New York

PAUL SIGNAC, French 1863–1935

French Art Galleries, New York

St. Tropez

EDOUARD MANET, French 1832–1883   The Guitarist
William Church Osborn, New York

59

EDOUARD MANET, French 1832–1883

The Metropolitan Museum of Art, New York

Boating

PAUL GAUGUIN, French 1848–1903   Tahitians with Mangoes

William Church Osborn, New York

HENRI MATISSE, French 1869–   Still Life
          Mr. and Mrs. LeRay Berdeau, Villa Today, Palm Beach

MARY CASSATT, American 1845–1926   Lady at the Tea Table
The Metropolitan Museum of Art, New York

63

PIERRE AUGUSTE RENOIR, French 1841–1919   Mme. Charpentier and Her Children
The Metropolitan Museum of Art, New York

GEORGES ROUAULT, French 1871–

Zak Art Gallery, Paris

Suburb

65

VAN GOGH, Dutch 1853–1890   Wildenstein & Co., New York

The Field of Corn

CAMILLE PISSARRO, French 1830–1903   Peasant Woman
National Gallery of Art, Washington, D. C.
Chester Dale Collection (Loan)

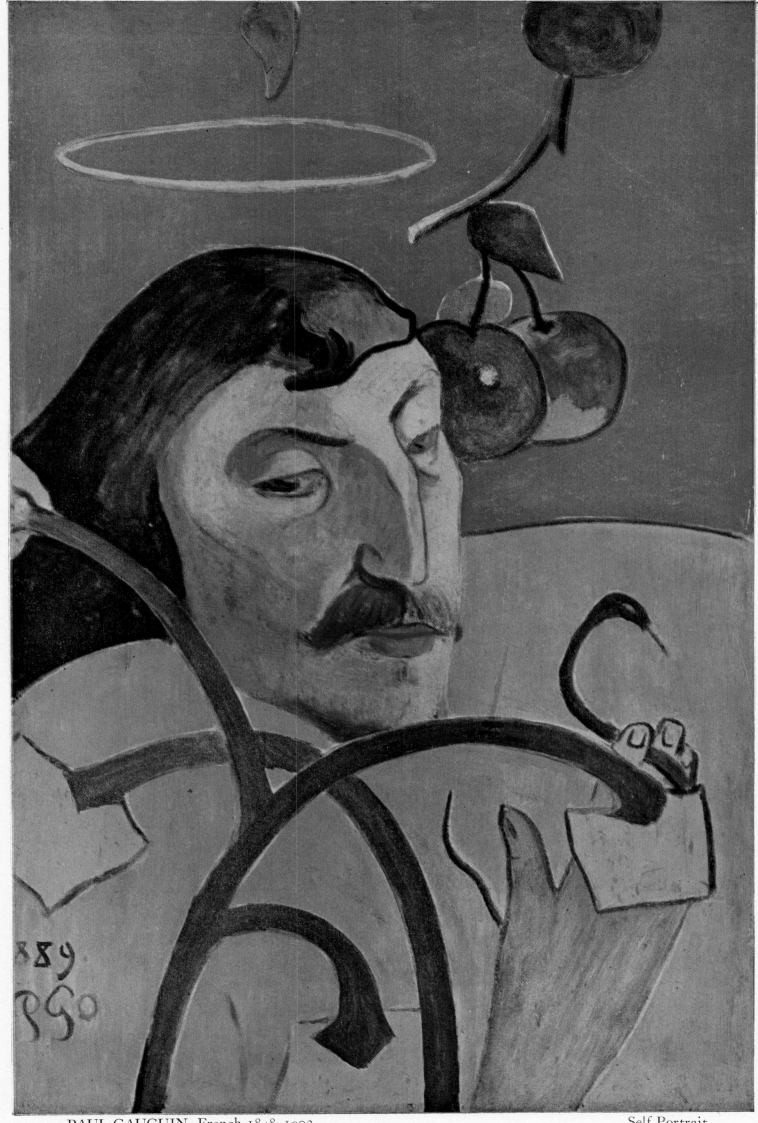

PAUL GAUGUIN, French 1848–1903   Self-Portrait

National Gallery of Art, Washington, D. C.
Chester Dale Collection (Loan)

PAUL CEZANNE, French 1839–1906   Vase of Flowers

National Gallery of Art, Washington, D. C.
Chester Dale Collection (Loan)

BERTHE MORISOT, French 1841–1895

In the Dining Room

National Gallery of Art, Washington, D. C.
Chester Dale Collection (Loan)

70

PIERRE AUGUSTE RENOIR, French 1841–1919   Mademoiselle Sicot
National Gallery of Art, Washington, D. C.
Chester Dale Collection (Loan)

71

PIERRE AUGUSTE RENOIR, French 1841-1919   **Girl with a Cat**
National Gallery of Art, Washington, D. C.
Whittemore Collection (Loan)

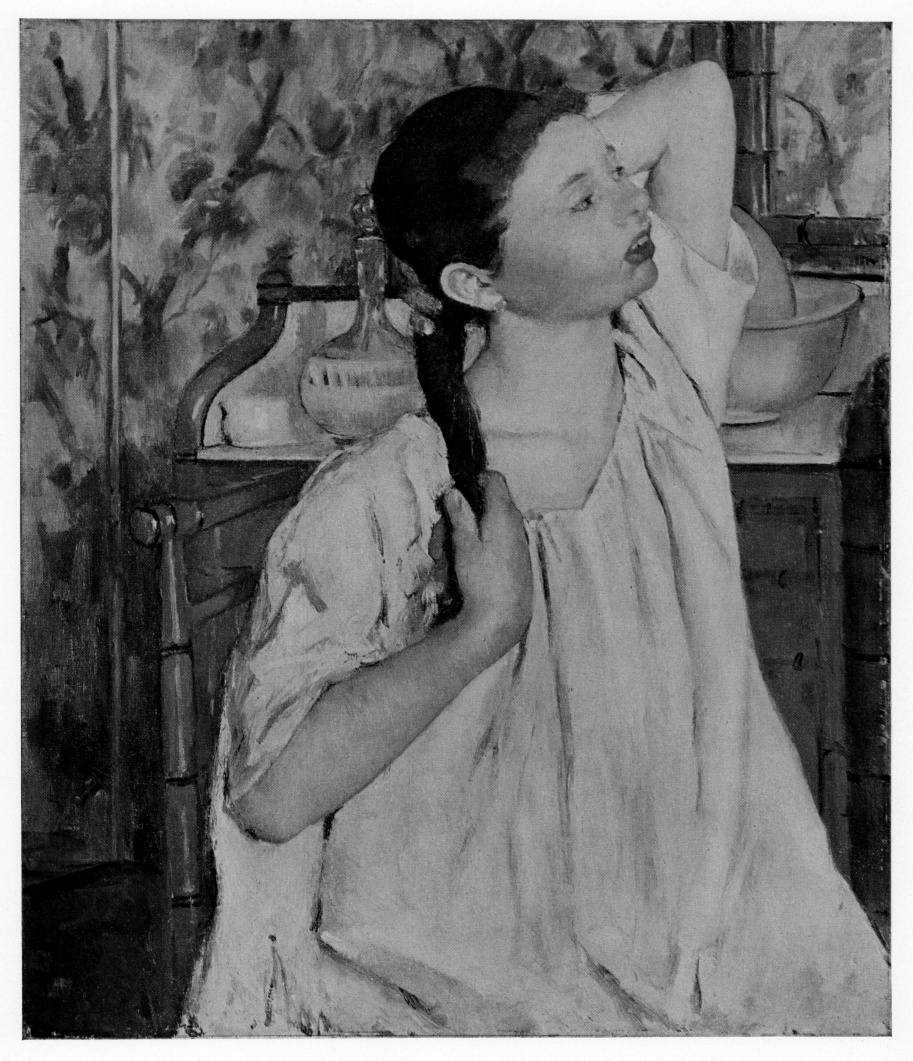

MARY CASSATT, American 1845–1926   The Morning Toilet
National Gallery of Art, Washington, D. C.
Chester Dale Collection (Loan)

PAUL CEZANNE, French 1839–1906   Man with a Straw Hat

The Metropolitan Museum of Art, New York

74

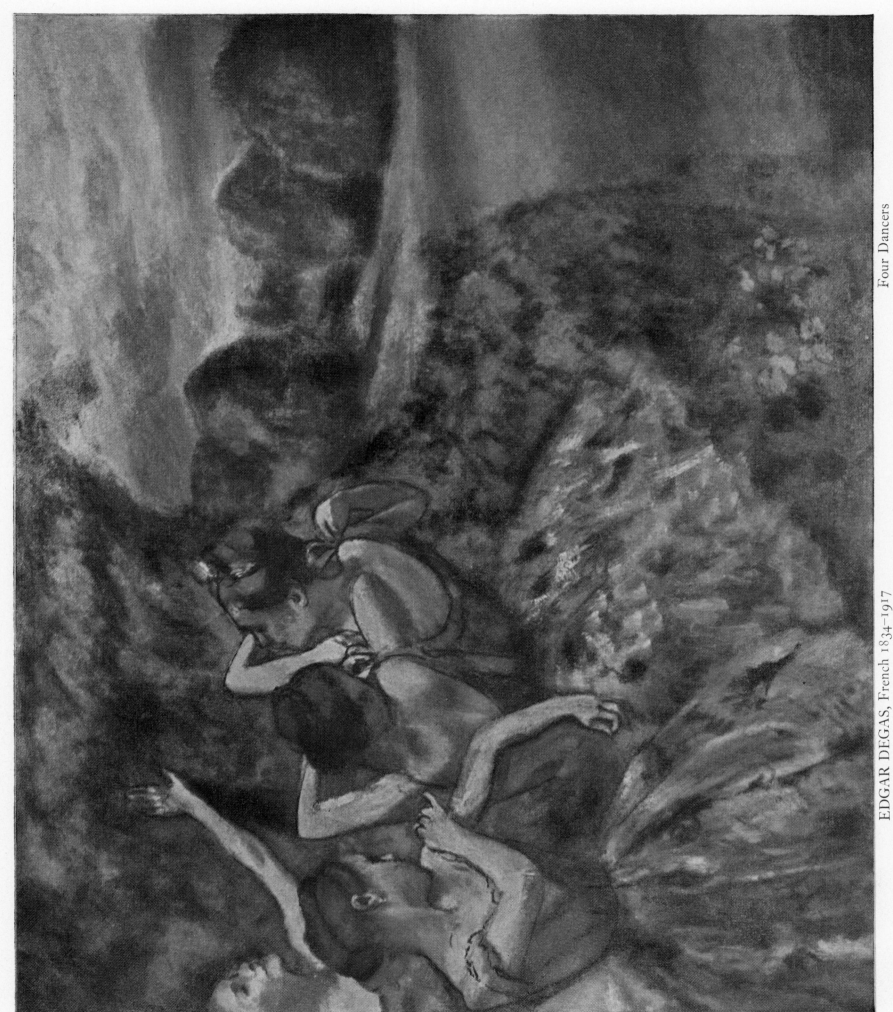

EDGAR DEGAS, French 1834–1917
National Gallery of Art, Washington, D. C.
Chester Dale Collection (Loan)

Four Dancers

GEORGE GROSZ, German 1893–   A Piece of My World   Associated American Artists Galleries, New York; Colorplate; Courtesy of Fortune Magazine

MARC CHAGALL, Russian 1887–ﾠ ﾠ ﾠThe Artist Angelﾠ ﾠ ﾠPrivate Collection; Colorplate: Courtesy of Harper's Bazaar Magazine

LOUIS EILSHEMIUS, American 1864–1941   Contentment   Kleemann Galleries, New York

JOHN STEUART CURRY, American 1897–   The Passing Leap
     Associated American Artists Galleries, New York
     Colorplate: Courtesy of Encyclopaedia Britannica   79

SALVADOR DALI, Spanish 1904–
Arthur Bradley Campbell, Palm Beach

Cardinal — Cardinal!

SALVADOR DALI, Spanish 1904–
Arthur Bradley Campbell, Palm Beach

Cardinal — Cardinal!

PAVEL TCHELITCHEW, Russian 1898–   Orchid Girl   Private Collection; Colorplate: Courtesy of Town & Country Magazine

PABLO PICASSO, Spanish 1881–

George L. K. Morris, New York

Head
82

GEORGES BRAQUE, French 1882–   Standing Woman

George L. K. Morris, New York   83

ENSIGN GEORGE F. HEUSTON, USMM, American 1906–

Australia

CORPORAL FRANK D. DUNCAN, JR., USA, American 1915–   Typical Rest Tent

TECHNICAL SERGEANT MANUEL BROMBERG, USA, American 1917–   The Card Players

FLETCHER MARTIN, American 1904–   Dancer Dressing
          Midtown Galleries, New York

YASUO KUNIYOSHI, American 1893–   All Alone

The Downtown Gallery, New York

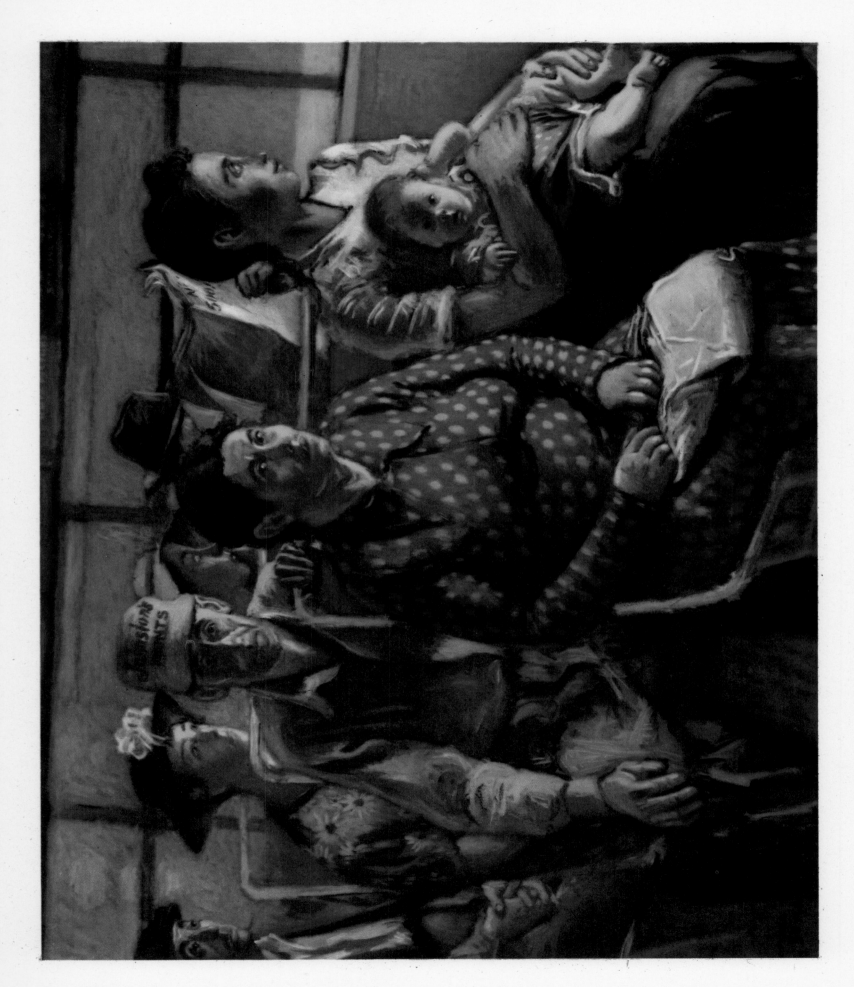

RAPHAEL SOYER, American 1899–
Collection Herman Shulman, Stamford, Conn.
Associated American Artists Galleries, New York

Bus Passengers

THOMAS HART BENTON, American 1889–
Collection and Colorplate: Abbott Laboratories, Chicago

New Year's Eve
90

GRANT WOOD, American 1892–1942   Adolescence
        Collection and Colorplate: Abbott Laboratories, Chicago   91

JOSE CLEMENTE OROZCO, Mexican 1883–
Mr. and Mrs. Louis Kaufman, Los Angeles

Cortez and Victory

92

HORACE PIPPIN, American 1888–   Harmonizing   The Downtown Gallery, New York

WALDO PEIRCE, American 1884–   Apple Pickers   Midtown Galleries, New York

DORIS ROSENTHAL, American Contemporary   Three Girls of Patzcuaro   Midtown Galleries, New York

EUGENE BERMAN, Russian 1899–
View in Perspective of a Perfect Sunset
Mr. and Mrs. Henry Clifford, Radnor, Pa.
Colorplate: Courtesy of Fortune Magazine

The City

FERNAND LEGER, French 1881–
Philadelphia Museum of Art; A. E. Gallatin Collection
Colorplate: Courtesy of Fortune Magazine

YVES TANGUY, French 1900–   Le Témoin

Mr. and Mrs. LeRay Berdeau, Villa Today, Palm Beach
Colorplate: Courtesy of Fortune Magazine

AUDREY BULLER, American 1902–   Morning Glory
The Metropolitan Museum of Art, New York

JACK LEVINE, American 1915–
The Metropolitan Museum of Art, New York

String Quartette